First World War
and Army of Occupation
War Diary
France, Belgium and Germany

27 DIVISION
Headquarters, Branches and Services
Royal Army Veterinary Corps
Assistant Director Veterinary Services
23 April 1915 - 31 December 1915

WO95/2256/5

The Naval & Military Press Ltd
www.nmarchive.com
Published in association with The National Archives

Published by

The Naval & Military Press Ltd

Unit 10 Ridgewood Industrial Park,

Uckfield, East Sussex,

TN22 5QE England

Tel: +44 (0) 1825 749494

www.naval-military-press.com

www.nmarchive.com

This diary has been reprinted in facsimile from the original. Any imperfections are inevitably reproduced and the quality may fall short of modern type and cartographic standards.

© **Crown Copyright**
Images reproduced by permission of The National Archives, London, England, 2015.

Contents

Document type	Place/Title	Date From	Date To
Heading	WO95/2256/5		
Heading	27th Division Divl Troops Asst Dir Vety Services. Apr-Dec 1915		
War Diary	Abeele	23/04/1915	23/04/1915
War Diary	Poperinghe	24/04/1915	25/04/1915
War Diary	Busseboom	26/04/1915	21/05/1915
War Diary	Ne Boeschepe	22/05/1915	30/05/1915
War Diary	Croix Au Bac	31/05/1915	31/05/1915
Heading	27th Division A.D.V.S. 27th Division Vol I 30.6.15		
War Diary	Croix Du Bac	01/06/1915	30/06/1915
Heading	27th Division A.D.V.S. 27th Division Vol II		
War Diary	Croix Du Bac	01/07/1915	30/07/1915
Heading	27th Division A.D.V.S. 27th Division Vol III From 29th July To 31st Aug 1915		
War Diary	Croix Du Bac	29/07/1915	31/08/1915
Heading	27th Division A.D.V.S. 27th Division Vol IV Sept 15		
War Diary	Croix Du Bac	01/09/1915	16/09/1915
War Diary	Merris	17/09/1915	18/09/1915
War Diary	Warfusee Abancourt	19/09/1915	21/09/1915
War Diary	Merricourt	22/09/1915	30/09/1915
Heading	A.D.V.S. 27th Division Vol V Oct 15		
War Diary	Mericourt	01/10/1915	29/10/1915
War Diary	Bouelles	30/10/1915	31/10/1915
Heading	A.D.V.S. 27th Div Nov 1915 Vol VI		
War Diary	Bovelles	01/11/1915	30/11/1915
Miscellaneous			
Heading	A.D.V.S. 27 Div Dec Vol VII		
War Diary	Bovelles	01/12/1915	09/12/1915
War Diary	Marseilles	10/12/1915	31/12/1915

WO95/2256/5

27TH DIVISION
DIVL TROOPS

ASST DIR VETY SERVICES.
APR - DEC 1915

WAR DIARY
or
INTELLIGENCE SUMMARY.
(Erase heading not required.)

27th Division Army Form C. 2118.

A D V S

Hour, Date, Place		Summary of Events and Information	Remarks and references to Appendices
23.4.15	ABEELE	Received orders to hand over No 5 Mobile Veterinary Section to Lt. HALSTEAD, and to join the 27th Division as A.D.V.S.	Apr 15. to Dec 15.
24.4.15	POPERINGHE	Proceeded to POPERINGHE. 27th D.H.Q at POTIJE E.of YPRES. The Q branch is split up on account of the shelling of YPRES. Found my clerk at No 16 M. A.D.M.S. + D.A.D.M.S. in POPERINGHE. Moved him + the office over to POPERINGHE. Obtained a Servant (Carpenter) from the M.V.S. Retained my annual + recent orders to remain at POPERINGHE. POPERINGHE shelled this afternoon.	
25.4.15	POPERINGHE	A.D.M.S. + my office shelled by a shell. Moved office to M.V.S. at BUSSEBOOM	
26.4.15	BUSSEBOOM	Inspected 1st Adv. R.F.A. Amm. Col. Saw Veterinary officers of the Division	
27.4.15	—	Inspected the Divisional Ammunition Column, Lts 19½ Ade Amm. Col.	

Army Form C. 2118.

WAR DIARY
or
INTELLIGENCE SUMMARY.
(Erase heading not required.)

Instructions regarding War Diaries and Intelligence Summaries are contained in F. S. Regs., Part II. and the Staff Manual respectively. Title pages will be prepared in manuscript.

Hour, Date, Place	Summary of Events and Information	Remarks and references to Appendices
28.4.15 BUSSEBOOM	Lt LUCAS arrived. Rode him to the 20th Bde. R.F.A. and to the Div. Train to enquire about his things from upon the Supply Column to move. Inspected the Divisional Train Supply Company. A Squadron.	
29.4.15 "	Inspected 1st Bde. R.F.A. Ammunition Column. Went round at 10 from. to send an N.C.O. & orderly to POTIJZE to allot R.A.H.Q. horse "Q" Branch now arrived at BUSSEBOOM. Scattered in farms. The distribution of Veterinary Officers in this division is not to each artillery Bde. The ammunition Col. are to the 3 Inf. Bdes. The Div. Train & Div Cavalry are attended to by the O.C. M.V.S. The officers attending the Inf. Bdes. is attached to their H.Q. This is practicable at present owing to the Infantry Transport being brigaded. Ipswich from home have been killed by Shells during the 20th April.	
30.4.15 "		

Bewell
Capt A.D.V.S.
2/6th

(73989) W4141—463. 400,000. 9/14. H.&J.Ltd. Forms/C. 2118/10.

27 Division
ADVS

Army Form C. 2118.

WAR DIARY
or
INTELLIGENCE SUMMARY.
(Erase heading not required.)

Instructions regarding War Diaries and Intelligence Summaries are contained in F.S. Regs., Part II. and the Staff Manual respectively. Title pages will be prepared in manuscript.

Hour, Date, Place	Summary of Events and Information	Remarks and references to Appendices
1.5.15 BUSSEBOOM.	Inspected the transport of the 81st & 82nd Infantry Brigades	
2.5.15 "	32 horses evacuated. Inspected all the horses of the Headquarter Staff, attended to several wounded.	
3.5.15 "	32 horses evacuated. Saw Lt PICKEY, HALFHEAD and HUNTER. Inspected the horses of the Divisional Train. Inspected a Section of the Div. Amm. Col.	
4.5.15 "	32 horses evacuated. Inspected the 11th Bde. R.G.A.	
5.5.15 "	32 horses evacuated. Inspected the 1st Bde. R.F.A., 1st Wessex Field Co, 1st Field Ambulance.	
6.5.15 "	Inspected the transport of the 60 to Infantry Brigade	
7.5.15 "	40 horses evacuated. Inspected the H.Q. fig Co & a Section of the Div. Amm. Col.	
8.5.15 "	Inspected Field Co R.E.	

Army Form C. 2118.

WAR DIARY
or
INTELLIGENCE SUMMARY.
(Erase heading not required.)

Instructions regarding War Diaries and Intelligence Summaries are contained in F.S. Regs., Part II. and the Staff Manual respectively. Title pages will be prepared in manuscript.

Hour, Date, Place	Summary of Events and Information	Remarks and references to Appendices
9.5.15 BUSSEBOOM	Inspected 81st & 82nd Field Ambulances	
10.5.15 "	" A.Q. Sig. Co. & 83rd Field Ambulance	
11.5.15 "	Some batteries of the 19th North Midland. R.F.A. Obtained several charges for N.O. of 6 Infantry Brigade orders	
12.5.15 "	Inspected 19th Bde. R.F.A.	
13.5.15 "	" 20th "	
14.5.15 "	" H.Q. Sig. Co. & 61st Battery R.F.A.	
15.5.15 "	Inspected Divisional Train	
16.5.15 "	" 81st Bde Infantry Transport	
17.5.15 "	Inspected 17 Co. R.E., 1 Wurm Co. R.E.	
18.5.15 "	H.Q. Sig. Co. & 19 Bde R.F.A. Ammn. Col. inspected	
19.5.15 "	Went to L.G. Div. H.Q. to arrange about 115 Bde R.G.A. being transferred to 4 F. Brown	
20.5.15 "	Inspected 2 Sects. Div. Ammn. Col.	

Army Form C. 2118.

WAR DIARY
or
INTELLIGENCE SUMMARY.
(Erase heading not required.)

Instructions regarding War Diaries and Intelligence Summaries are contained in F.S. Regs., Part II. and the Staff Manual respectively. Title pages will be prepared in manuscript.

Hour, Date, Place	Summary of Events and Information	Remarks and references to Appendices
21.5.15 BUSSEBOOM	Received orders to move the M.V.S. from BUSSEBOOM to rear of Divisional area to make room for Infantry coming in to reserve. Went to find a farm forward on the BOESCHEPE - POPER- INGHE road. The Section moved into the new billet during the evening. Left a party to collect any horses that might come in to-day and to-morrow. Relieved rear portion of Divisional orders	
22.5.15 Nr BOESCHEPE	Inspected H.Q. Signal Co. & 81st Field Ambulance	
23.5.15 " "	Saw Lt. HALFHEAD - HUNTER	
24.5.15 " "	11th Bde. R.F.A. transferred to the 4.5 Division for administration. Saw Capt. SYMES.	
25.5.15 " "	Went to addresses to see entrainment of horses. Inspected H.Q. Sig. Co. — Sergt. Yeomanry	
26.5.15 " "	Saw 19th Bde. R.F.A.	
27.5.15 " "	Had a conversation with O.C. Train about the Phoenix of	

Fy Patterson

(73989) W4141—463. 400,000. 9/14. H.&J.Ltd. Forms/C. 2118/10.

Army Form C. 2118.

WAR DIARY
or
INTELLIGENCE SUMMARY.
(Erase heading not required.)

Instructions regarding War Diaries and Intelligence Summaries are contained in F.S. Regs., Part II. and the Staff Manual respectively. Title pages will be prepared in manuscript.

Hour, Date, Place	Summary of Events and Information	Remarks and references to Appendices
28.5.15. M. BOESCHEPE.	The 27th Div. is about to move into a new area with D.D.V.S. of M.V.S. to be about billets in arranged stables now being occupied by No 6 M.V.S. moving out with D.H.Q.	
29.5.15 "	Made arrangements to join D.H.Q. again an advance in new area. The D.H.Q. in new area will be in a village yet will be possible for every horse to be together again. Section evacuated all horses — to move to new area to-morrow all the wounded with two left.	
30.5.15 "		
31.5.15 Croix du BAC	Moved to the new area. Section installed in new billet. Arrangements were being made to dig wells. The move then I moved little to D.H.Q. Inspected M.V.S. fell away with the recent influx. (1) The question of the water supply was becoming serious in the old area. Arrangements were being made to dig wells. (2) 466 horses were destroyed by Shells during the month. 306 have been evacuated by the M.V.S. (mostly shell wounds.) The Section has been kept at in high pressure the relief of much needed.	

Army Form C. 2118.

WAR DIARY
or
INTELLIGENCE SUMMARY.
(Erase heading not required.)

Instructions regarding War Diaries and Intelligence Summaries are contained in F.S. Regs., Part II. and the Staff Manual respectively. Title pages will be prepared in manuscript.

Hour, Date, Place	Summary of Events and Information	Remarks and references to Appendices
31.5.15 CROIX DU BAC	of the large number of sick amongst has amply demonstrated the greatness of the M.V.S. (3) The shoeing of Infantry transport is a question which has supplied considerable attention during the month. Local schools have been established when the Supervision of the former of the Bn. Transport to instruct cold shoers of infantry in fitting shoes but ratio in instruction sent men in cold shoeing. The shoes of the Infantry Transport has been very beneficial results the average Infantry Transport has by much attain (4) The condition of the horses of the Division, with the exception of 2 batteries & one Bde. Amm. Col. is remarkably good the horses of the Infantry Transport are in very good condition indeed. B. wrote Capt A.V.S. 27.M.D.	

(73989) W4141—463. 400,000. 9/14. H.&J.Ltd. Forms/C. 2118/10.

121/5829

27th Division

A.D.V.S. 27th Division

23.4 — 30.6.15.

WAR DIARY
or
INTELLIGENCE SUMMARY.
(Erase heading not required.)

Army Form C. 2118.

Hour, Date, Place	Summary of Events and Information	Remarks and references to Appendices
1.6.15 CROIX DU BAC	Wrote V.O. Div. Amm. Col. 5th Officer i/c charge of the 81st Field Ambulance. In Morn C.R.E., 2nd Section No 2 Fortifying Party, & Armourable Heavy Battery. Saw A.D.M.S. about a car. Handed in an application through the G.O.C. Wrote my strength recommended same. Saw C.R.A. C.R.E. about new units in the area. The 12th Hour Bde & the 19th Infantry Brigade are now attached to this division. There is a V.O. with two in the Hour. Bde. (He also looks after the 19th) I.B. If there is a Hour. Bde. more, then will be no one with the 19th I.B. Inspected M.V.S.	
2.6.15 " "	The 19th I.B. Inspected H.Q. Sig. Co. & 2nd Sect. Bridging Train.	
3.6.15 " "	It is impossible for the V.O. of this bde. to live at Div. H.Q. as it is too far away from the Tpt. Transport. I lent him a horse to ride. He has left to live in ARMENTIÈRES. Inspected 20th Bde. A.C.	
4.6.15 " "	Inspected the 19th T.M. Bdes A.C.	
5.6.15 " "	Inspected 1st Bde. A.C.	

Army Form C. 2118.

WAR DIARY
or
INTELLIGENCE SUMMARY.
(Erase heading not required.)

Instructions regarding War Diaries and Intelligence Summaries are contained in F.S. Regs., Part II. and the Staff Manual respectively. Title pages will be prepared in manuscript.

Hour, Date, Place	Summary of Events and Information	Remarks and references to Appendices
6.6.15 CROIX DU BAC	Inspected M.V.S. HQ Sig Co	
7.6.15 "	Inspected the horses of the 82nd I. Bde & 174 C.R.E. Saw O.C. 19 A.C. arranged to inspect horses of the Brigade tomorrow	
8.6.15 "	Inspected the 19th F.A. Brigade	
9.6.15 "	" 80 & 81st Infantry Brigade horses	
10.6.15 "	Saw A.Q. Sig Co	
11.6.15 "	Saw O.C. 19th Bde R.F.A.	
12.6.15 "	—	
13.6.15 "	Inspected horses at M.V.S.	
14.6.15 "	Inspected Warwick Heavy Battery. 16th Bde R.G.A., which together with the 115th Htt Battery form Currie's Group. Lt RICHARDSON is in Veterinary charge of the 16th Bde R.G.A. The 115th H.B. is in 4th Divisional area. Three now form front of the Battery	

WAR DIARY
or
INTELLIGENCE SUMMARY.
(Erase heading not required.)

Army Form C. 2118.

Instructions regarding War Diaries and Intelligence Summaries are contained in F.S. Regs., Part II. and the Staff Manual respectively. Title pages will be prepared in manuscript.

Hour, Date, Place	Summary of Events and Information	Remarks and references to Appendices
15.6.15 CROIX DU BAC	Went to inspect 12th Bde R.F.A. Was informed that they were rejoining the 6th Division. This unit was taken V.O. from the 19 I.B. 19 field Ambulance, 19.5 Train, & 19 I.B. Amm. Col., without a Veterinary officer. Saw V.O. 20th Bde. R.F.A. & told him to take on charge of the 19 I.B. Yatrined troops in addition to his present duties. Wrote about motor car to D.A.V.S.	
16.6.15 CROIX DU BAC	Saw A.A. & Q.M.G. about a fellow into M.V.S. Inspected the Div. Train.	
17.6.15 " "	Saw G.S.O. 2 & arranged about a rifle range for rifle practice into M.V.S.	
18.6.15 " "	Inspected the Divisional Ammunition Column. Went to ARMENTIÈRES, Saw Staff Captain of the 6th Inf. Bde. & arranged for the range for the 21st for use of the H.V.S.	
19.6.15 " "	Saw H.Q. Sig. Co.	

Army Form C. 2118.

WAR DIARY
or
INTELLIGENCE SUMMARY.
(Erase heading not required.)

Instructions regarding War Diaries and Intelligence Summaries are contained in F.S. Regs., Part II and the Staff Manual respectively. Title pages will be prepared in manuscript.

Hour, Date, Place	Summary of Events and Information	Remarks and references to Appendices
20.6.15 CROIX DU BAC.	Inspected detachment 2o in Bolton Co R.E.	
21.6.15 "	Inspected gth Co of the Train 17th Co. R.E.	
22.6.15 "	Inspected the horses of the 19th Inf. Bde, 19th Field Ambulance 19th Train, & 19th Bde. Amm Col. Saw Lt Col HUNTER & RICHARDSON about certain cases	
23.6.15 "		
24.6.15 "	Inspected Remount 1/the 19.5. & 1st Bde R.F.A. visited the headquarters of Currie Group = A Group R.F.A. This Group has one battery from each of the 1st & 19th Bdes R.F.A. & an additional battery A63 attached. With 27 he this took telegram to the 9th division.	
25.6.15 "	" "	
26.6.15 "	" "	
27.6.15 "	" & inspected H.Q. Sy. Co.	

WAR DIARY
or
INTELLIGENCE SUMMARY.
(Erase heading not required.)

Army Form C. 2118.

Hour, Date, Place	Summary of Events and Information	Remarks and references to Appendices
26.6.15 CROIX DU BAC	Reinspected 1st Bde. R.F.A. remounts. Simple report on them	
29.6.15	Inspected Remounts of 2nd Bde R.F.A., also 3 horses kept with the Bgdr of (?) Division. They are Cavs. (Arranged (in train deliveries delivery) GOC HQ Co tow. Train (in reserve) Wrote to 82 I.B. A.Q. to arrange about the rifle range. In the M.V.S. on June 1st. Inspected the remounts of the Royal Irish Rgt. Saw horses at M.V.C.	
30.6.15 "	(1) The condition of the horses is very good indeed. The brigades Amm. Col., & the 2 batteries previously mentioned have now greatly improved. (2) A rain arrangy through the Divisional area has been solved the problem of water supply completely. (3) A car is absolutely essential in the efficient veterinary attendance of the Division. The V.O. Inf. Bdes must have	

Army Form C. 2118.

WAR DIARY
or
INTELLIGENCE SUMMARY.
(Erase heading not required.)

Instructions regarding War Diaries and Intelligence Summaries are contained in F.S. Regs., Part II and the Staff Manual respectively. Title pages will be prepared in manuscript.

Hour, Date, Place	Summary of Events and Information	Remarks and references to Appendices
30.6.15. CROIX DU BAC	The use of a car, which should bring together A.V.S. the strength of this division has been increased by one bde. Bde. attached troops, mostly 4 Inf. Bdes. In addition there are a large number of small units in the div. area which require veterinary attendance with the by addition better strength of the division is a reduction of 4 officers in the normal establishment. (ii) Owing to the sentence of the front line Transport of the Inf. Bdes. from the temporary of the Train, it is impossible, except in one case, to provide for instruction. Arrangements are being made to send some men to the School at G.H.Q. Manro Capt. A.D.V.S. 27/Div.	

27th Division

121/6306

A.D.V.S. 27th Division

Vol II

Army Form C. 2118.

WAR DIARY
or
INTELLIGENCE SUMMARY.
(Erase heading not required.)

Instructions regarding War Diaries and Intelligence Summaries are contained in F.S. Regs., Part II. and the Staff Manual respectively. Title pages will be prepared in manuscript.

Hour, Date, Place	Summary of Events and Information	Remarks and references to Appendices
1.7.15 CROIX DU BAC	Inspected H.Q. Sig. Co. M.V.S. went to rifle range & attend charter practice by N.C.O.s seven of the M.V.S. Sent O.C. 1st Bde. R.F.A. Inspected 13th Batter 1st Bde.	
2.7.15 " "	Made an experiment to discover whether horses & mules would drink water that has been treated with Kerosene oil to prevent the breeding of mosquitoes. They betrayed no aversion to such water. Inspected all horses at A.H.Q.	
3.7.15 " "	Visited 19th Bde. R.F.A. HQ. 79th Bde. R.F.A. Amm. Col. Sent D.A.V.S.	
4.7.15 " "		
5.7.15 " "	10am saw the M.V.S. from O.C., proceeding on leave.	
6.7.15 " "	Inspected D.A.C. 81st M.F.A. 1st Bde. R.E., 20th Indian Co. R.E. Pridging Train & went to M.V.C. Survey Thomsons ad inoculed Train.	

Army Form C. 2118.

WAR DIARY
or
INTELLIGENCE SUMMARY.
(Erase heading not required.)

Instructions regarding War Diaries and Intelligence Summaries are contained in F.S. Regs., Part II. and the Staff Manual respectively. Title pages will be prepared in manuscript.

Hour, Date, Place	Summary of Events and Information	Remarks and references to Appendices
7.7.15 Croix do Bac	Saw H Phipps A.V.C.	
8.7.15 "	"	
9.7.15 "	Saw H. Richardson. A.V.C.	
10.7.15 "	Inspected Divisional Train & Yeomanry. Visited the H.V.S.	
11.7.15 "	Sundry applications for a car. Rearranged distribution of V.O.s in the Division.	
12.7.15 "	Inspected Div. Train Essex Yeomanry. Visited M.V.S.	
13.7.15 "	ditto	
14.7.15 "	O.C. M.V.S. returned from leave, handed over to him attention of Divisional area, necessitating a further rearrangement of V.O.s. D.D.R. cast horses at H.Q. Co. Train attended same.	
15.7.15 "	Inspected M.V.S.	

Army Form C. 2118.

WAR DIARY
or
INTELLIGENCE SUMMARY.
(Erase heading not required.)

Instructions regarding War Diaries and Intelligence Summaries are contained in F.S. Regs., Part II. and the Staff Manual respectively. Title pages will be prepared in manuscript.

Hour, Date, Place	Summary of Events and Information	Remarks and references to Appendices
16.7.15 CROIX DU BAC	M.V.S. moved to new billet. Arranged some new O.C. Train about supply of munchies out.	
17.7.15 " "	Handed on O.M. JORNSUCC. Proceeded on leave. Brunon transferred to 1st Army siege	
18.7.15 " "	A.D.V.S. I both Armies	
" "	2nd Mountain Battery joined the Division	
19.7.15 " "	B.H.Q. horses inspected	
20.7.15 " "	19th I.B. Train inspected	
21.7.15 " "	5th Heavy Bde. R.G.A inspected. Joined Division in place of 16th Bde. R.G.A.	
22.7.15 " "	19th L.F. Bde & 170 C.R.C. left the Division	
23.7.15 " "	Inspection of Bridges Train	
24.7.15 " "	82nd F.A. Shown inspected, reported unfit. Alterations proposed.	

WAR DIARY
or
INTELLIGENCE SUMMARY.

(Erase heading not required.)

Army Form C. 2118.

Instructions regarding War Diaries and Intelligence Summaries are contained in F. S. Regs., Part II. and the Staff Manual respectively. Title pages will be prepared in manuscript.

Hour, Date, Place	Summary of Events and Information	Remarks and references to Appendices
25.7.15 CROIX DU BAC	Remonstration of the intradermal mallein test at H.Q. 9th Division. V.Os attended.	
26.7.15 "	Capt. DANIELS returned from leave. Lieut new from M. TURNBULL	
27.7.15 "	Inspected M.S. & G.M. 4.A. Received orders to proceed to LONDON & report to Head Office on relief by MAJOR BOSELEY.	
28.7.15 "	The removal of the 19th I.B. Econometric V.O.s & a new district structure arrangement will be provided. The will be come into force from tomorrow. The 2 Mountain Batts, upon this Division in turn, 1 Section (which	
29.7.15 "	Inspected on arrival of Kind Plate etc. Satisfactory. Major J. A. BOSELEY Ave arrived to take over.	
30.7.15 "	Handing over to the above.	Danielo Capt. A.V.C.

121/6550

27th Division

A.D.V.S. 27th Division
Pt III
from 29th July to 31st Aug. 1915

Army Form C. 2118.

WAR DIARY
or
INTELLIGENCE SUMMARY.
(Erase heading not required.)

Instructions regarding War Diaries and Intelligence Summaries are contained in F.S.Regs., Part II. and the Staff Manual respectively. Title pages will be prepared in manuscript.

Hour, Date, Place	Summary of Events and Information	Remarks and references to Appendices
July 29/15. Croix du Bac	Arrived Croix du Bac 4 p.m. Reported to D.A.Q.M.G. & A.D.V.S. 27th Division.	
July 30/15 "	Reported to G.O.C. 27th Division. Took over duties of A.D.V.S. 27th Div. from CAPT. DANELS, A.V.C. Reported arrival by letter to D.D.V.S. 1st Army & D.A.Q.M.G.	
July 31/15 "	Read through Office correspondence with CAPT. DANELS, A.V.C. Studied Routine & Standing Orders that had been published by Gen. French during the campaign. Inspected with (late) CAPT. DANELS No. 16 M.V. Section.	
Aug 1/15 "	CAPT. DANELS, A.V.C. left for England. Inspected 4th Signal Co. R.E. M.M.P. horses. 364 Battery. Saw D.D.V.S. 1st Army.	
Aug 2/15 "	Inspected 51st Field Ambulance horses & 9/5 W.A.S.C. The whole morning taken up inspecting two units on account of the distance. No motor car allotted to A.D.V.S. this division. LIEUT. PHIPPS A.V.C. left for LAHORE CAVALRY DIV. Reported his departure to D.D.V.S. 1st Army & D.A.Q.M.G. this division	

Army Form C. 2118.

WAR DIARY
or
INTELLIGENCE SUMMARY.
(Erase heading not required.)

Instructions regarding War Diaries and Intelligence Summaries are contained in F.S. Regs., Part II and the Staff Manual respectively. Title pages will be prepared in manuscript.

Hour, Date, Place	Summary of Events and Information	Remarks and references to Appendices
Aug 3/15. Croix du Bac	Inspected 2nd Wessex Co. R.G. & Headquarters horses. Sent instructions for all V.Os. the division to meet at A.D.V.S' office at 3p.m on Friday to discuss professional routine matters such as shoeing, feeding etc. Received Telegram LIEUT. REID. A.V.C. will & 4t. sw. Transferred to 27t. sw. for duty.	
Aug 4/15. " "	Capt. GRIGNON, in Veterinary charge Canadian heavy Battery, reported his arrival, on coming temporarily into the divisional area. Inspected 95 Bty. 39 Bty. 96 Bty. 131 Bty. A 53 Bty. & A 53 Amm Col. with LIEUT. HALFHEAD. A.V.C.	
Aug 5/15 " "	Saw B.O.C. Inspected 1st Canadian Heavy Bty. with CAPT. GRIGNON. Inspected 50t Infantry Brigade with LIEUT. NICHOLAS A.V.C.	
Aug 6/15	Inspected 119th Bty, Warwick Amm. Col., West-Riding Ammun. Col., 1st Glamorgan Field Co. R.E. Held meeting of all V. Os. in div. Instructed them to lecture & explain to Company shoeing staff the regulations & methods of Army shoeing. All Officers attended except Lieut. Hunter.	

Army Form C. 2118.

WAR DIARY
or
INTELLIGENCE SUMMARY.
(Erase heading not required.)

Instructions regarding War Diaries and Intelligence Summaries are contained in F.S. Regs., Part II and the Staff Manual respectively. Title pages will be prepared in manuscript.

Hour, Date, Place	Summary of Events and Information	Remarks and references to Appendices
Aug 7/15. Gorre du Bac	With G.O.C. to inspect No 1 B.M.V.S. Visited Supply Officer re forage Copy of circ. memo no 39 sent to all R.Os. (number cases of various diseases)	
Aug 8/15 " "	Inspected 39 Bty. 95 Bty. Gloster Rgt. & 1st Argyll & Suth. H'rdrs transport. Sent memo to all R.Os re punctuality of weekly return. Memo. to all R.Os not to clip legs as routine measure.	
Aug 9/15 " "	Inspected with Capt. SYMES (R O i/c) & COL. BOUVRIE (C.O) Divisional Ammn. Column & 82 Field Ambulance	
Aug 10/15 " "	Saw G.O.C. Inspected Surrey Yeomanry. Sent Circ. memo nos. 2 & 3 all R.Os. re shoeing & duties.	
Aug 11/15. " "	Inspected 20th Brigade Ammn Col. Sent circ. memo to all R.Os. (where to be found in emergency). Inspected 96 Co A.S.C.	
Aug 12/15. " "	Inspected 133 Bty. 132 Bty. 114th Bty. 1st Wessex Co R.E. with LIEUT. HUNTER. A.V.C	
Aug 13/15. " "	Inspected 2nd Wessex Co R.E., 17th Co R.E. LIEUT. REID reported his arrival at 3.45 p.m. Sent to take over S.V.O. duties to 82nd Infantry Brigades.	

Army Form C. 2118.

WAR DIARY
or
INTELLIGENCE SUMMARY.
(Erase heading not required.)

Instructions regarding War Diaries and Intelligence Summaries are contained in F.S. Regs., Part II. and the Staff Manual respectively. Title pages will be prepared in manuscript.

Hour, Date, Place	Summary of Events and Information	Remarks and references to Appendices
Aug 14/15 Guinchy du Bac.	Doing weekly returns.	
Aug 15/15 "	Attended conference of all Staff & Heads of Septs. held by G.O.C. Published surviving Order re Clipping. Rained.	
Aug 16/15 "	Inspected 67 Bty, 364 Bty, 148 Bty, 99 Bty, 98 Bty, C65 Bty with LIEUTS. HUNTER & LUCAS.	
Aug 17/15 "	Inspected 1st Brigade Ammunition Col., 95 Co. A.S.C.	
Aug 18/15 "	Called a meeting of all Officers A.V.C. for next Friday afternoon. Inspected 96 Co. A.S.C., 81st Infantry Transport	
Aug 19/15 "	Inspected 97 Co. A.S.C., 19th Bde Ammun. Col., 83 Field Ambulance	
Aug 20/15 "	Inspected No 16 M.V.S. Headquarters Signal Co R.E. Held meeting of Officers A.V.C. 27th Div. All attended.	
Aug 21/15 "	Inspected 39 Y Bty. Divcl Transport. Saw D.D.V.S. 1st Army. Lieut. NICHOLAS A.V.C. 1/c 8th Heavy Brigade R.S.A. temporarily in sui Area left. Inoculated against Enteric (1st)	

Army Form C. 2118.

WAR DIARY
or
INTELLIGENCE SUMMARY.
(Erase heading not required.)

Instructions regarding War Diaries and Intelligence Summaries are contained in F.S. Regs., Part II. and the Staff Manual respectively. Title pages will be prepared in manuscript.

Hour, Date, Place	Summary of Events and Information	Remarks and references to Appendices
Aug 22/15 Croix du Bac.	Weekly returns & Office work.	
Aug 23/15 "	Inspected 20 Lorries Co R.E. 82nd Field Ambulance. 9th Royal Scots. 1st Royal Scots. 67 Battery. Applied for a car, obtained it with the request not to keep it long. Inspection hurried.	
Aug 24/15 "	Interviewed G.O.C. Inspected Surrey Yeomanry.	
Aug 25/15 "	Inspected 2/Royal Fusiliers. 1/Cambridge Rgt. 1/Lemolis R.Scots Rgt. D.C.L.I.? Applied for car - couldn't obtain it.	
Aug 26/15 "	Inspected 367 Bty. Applied for car, obtained it. Saw 3.O.C 82nd Infantry Brigade re horses manure (disposal of) Inspected 82nd Bde Transport.	
Aug 27/15 "	Inspected 98 & 99 Batts. with Divisional Artillery Commander. Inspected 364 with Brigade Commander.	
Aug 28/15 "	Interviewed G.O.C. Inspected 98 Co A.S.C. D.D.R. held casting Board - attended.	
Aug 29/15 "	Inspected O/92 Battery. Hdqrs 129 Brigade Artillery. 1st Royal Scots. 9th Battery. Applied for car, obtained it.	

Army Form C. 2118.

WAR DIARY
or
INTELLIGENCE SUMMARY.
(Erase heading not required.)

Instructions regarding War Diaries and Intelligence Summaries are contained in F. S. Regs., Part II and the Staff Manual respectively. Title pages will be prepared in manuscript.

Hour, Date, Place	Summary of Events and Information	Remarks and references to Appendices
Aug 30/15. Cuin du Bac.	At Mobile V.S. Went with A.D.M.S. on a sanitary inspection	
Aug 31/15 " "	Inspected 4th K.R.R. K.S.L.I. Second inoculation for Enteric. Saw D.D.V.S. 1st Army. Sent circ: memo. to all Officers A.V.C. asking them to collect ends of all empty unit-chests bearing our distinguishing mark. Wanted for advanced dressing station & dressing posts etc.	

J. W. Moseley Major A.V.C.

Headquarters
27 Div.
31 Aug/15

12/7051

27th Division

A.D.V.S. 27th Division

Vol IV

Sept. 15

WAR DIARY of A.D.V.S. 27th Division

Army Form C. 2118.

Instructions regarding War Diaries and Intelligence Summaries are contained in F.S. Regs., Part II. and the Staff Manual respectively. Title pages will be prepared in manuscript.

INTELLIGENCE SUMMARY.
(Erase heading not required.)

Hour, Date, Place	Summary of Events and Information	Remarks and references to Appendices
Sept. 1/15, Gwia du Bac.	Fever.	
Sept. 2/15 "	Inspected 19th Bde Ammun. Col. with Brigade Major. Divisional Artillery	
Sept. 3/15 "	Rained all day. Worked out scheme for advanced collecting stations & line of evacuation for disabled horses. Drew map & marked places with the roads. Submitted scheme to D.D.V.S. 1st Army + Q.	
Sept. 4/15 "	At M.V.S. Attended conference of all A.D.V.S. held by D.D.V.S. 1st Army.	
Sept. 5/15 "	Inspected 1st Bridging Train. Divisional Ammun. Col.	
Sept. 6/15 "	Inspected Warwick Bty & Ammun. Col. 115 Bty R.G.A.	
Sept. 7/15 "	Inspected Shoeing Smith at work in central forge. Saw D.D.V.S. 1st Army	
Sept. 8/15 "	Inspected 115 Bty R.G.A. 99 Bty R.F.A. Inspected transport with O.C. Divisional Train.	
Sept. 9/15 "	Inspected 1st Brigade Ammun Co.	
Sept. 10/15 "	Inspected 141 Bty R.G.A. 96 Coy A.S.C. Interviewed O.C. 102, 104 & 105 Batteries. Applied for car, obtained it.	
Sept. 11/15 "	Inspected 1/Wessex to R.E. Bridging Train. 67 Bty 99 Bty 141 Bty 361 Bty. Saw D.D.V.S. 1st Army	
Sept. 12/15 "	Inspected 9th Yorks. Lancs. Leinsters, Royal Irish Fusiliers, Royal Irish Rgt. Transport.	
Sept. 13/15 "	Inspected 67 Bty, 34 Bty, 2/Wessex Co R.E. Lieut. STARKEY, A.V.C. reported his arrival in the Divisional Area yesterday	

WAR DIARY
or
INTELLIGENCE SUMMARY.
(Erase heading not required.)

Army Form C. 2118.

Instructions regarding War Diaries and Intelligence Summaries are contained in F.S. Regs., Part II. and the Staff Manual respectively. Title pages will be prepared in manuscript.

Hour, Date, Place	Summary of Events and Information	Remarks and references to Appendices
Sept. 14/15 Croix du Bac	Went to see A.D.V.S. 23rd Div on changing areas. Inspected 14 & Hy B.5. R.G.A.	
Sept. 15/15 " " "	Inspected 19th Bde R.F.A.	
Sept. 16/15 " " "	Division moved to MERRIS by road.	
Sept. 17/15 MERRIS	At M.V.S. Arranging moves.	
Sept. 18/15 "	Division moved to Warfusée Abancourt by train. Proceeded by car with A.D.M.S.	
Sept. 19/15 WARFUSÉE ABANCOURT	Reconnoitred new area & chose site for M.V.S.	
Sept. 20/15 " "	Met M.V.S. at Station & showed them to their new position	
Sept. 21/15 " "	Division moved to MERRICOURT.	
Sept. 22/15 MERRICOURT	Saw D.D.V.S. 3rd Army. Inspected 95 Co. A.S.C. 1/Cambs. Regt & 97 Co. A.S.C.	
Sept. 23/15 " "	Inspected Div. Ammun Col. Applied for car. Obtained it with request not to keep it long.	
Sept. 24/15 " "	Rained. Inspected 81st Field Amb.	
Sept. 25/15 " "	Rained. Visited 1st Bde Ammun Col. 9 & 73 H & F.5. Held conference of all V.O.s.	
Sept. 26/15 " "	Went round divisional area & made a list of all civilian forges.	
Sept. 27/15 " "	Inspected Div. Train. Sent in memo no 7 to see r.o.s. re instruction re standing animal left behind on road. Rained.	
	Rained. Visited 1/1/133rd A.B. & C. B.5. 2nd Canadian Hy B.5. Applied for a car. Couldn't get our own.	

Army Form C. 2118.

WAR DIARY
or
INTELLIGENCE SUMMARY.
(Erase heading not required.)

Hour, Date, Place	Summary of Events and Information	Remarks and references to Appendices
Sept. 28/15 MERRICOURT	Issued circ. memo no 8 to all V.Os re medicines not to be purchased locally. Inspected 2/Canadian Heavy Battery. Report on 15y GDBVS.	
Sept 29/15 "	Inspected K.S.L.I., 4th K.R.R.	
Sept 30/15 "	Inspected 129 Ammun. Col. & 2/Canadian Heavy Battery	

JapScally Major V.C.
A.D.V.S.
27th Division

121/7341

A.D.V.S. 27th Division

Vol V

Oct 15

Army Form C. 2118.

WAR DIARY
or
INTELLIGENCE SUMMARY.
(Erase heading not required.)

Instructions regarding War Diaries and Intelligence Summaries are contained in F.S. Regs., Part II and the Staff Manual respectively. Title pages will be prepared in manuscript.

Hour, Date, Place	Summary of Events and Information	Remarks and references to Appendices
Oct. 1/15 MERICOURT	Inspected 2nd Canadian Heavy Battery with D.D.V.S. 3rd Army	
Oct. 2/15 "	Inspected 2nd Canadian Heavy Battery with Brig. Gen. 12th Corps.	
Oct. 3/15 "	Inspected 129 Ammun. Col. Div. Ammun. Col. " " 108 Co. R.E.	
Oct. 4/15 "	Attended conference held by G.O.C. division. Inspected 2/ C. Highlanders & 9/ Royal Scots.	
Oct. 5/15 "	Inspected 97 & 98 Cos. A.S.C.	
Oct. 6/15 "	Inspected 95 Co. A.S.C. 1/A & S. Highlanders	
Oct. 7/15 "	Inspected P.P.C.L.I. R. Irish Fusiliers	
Oct. 8/15 "	81st, 82nd, 83rd Field Ambulances inspected	
Oct. 9/15 "	Inspected 133 Bty, 132 Bty, 98 Bty, A & B.Bde. 12 Bde.	
Oct. 10/15 "	Inspected Canadian Hy Bty. 96 Co. A.S.C.	
Oct. 11/15. "	Office work. Saw G.O.C.	
Oct. 12/15. "	Inspected 96 Bty, 131 Bty, 39 Bty, 95 Bty.	
Oct. 13/15 "	at M.V.S.	
Oct. 14/15 "	Inspected 189 Co. A.S.C.	
Oct. 15/15. "	Went to Railhead re arrival of medicines.	

Army Form C. 2118.

WAR DIARY
or
INTELLIGENCE SUMMARY.
(Erase heading not required.)

Instructions regarding War Diaries and Intelligence Summaries are contained in F.S. Regs., Part II. and the Staff Manual respectively. Title pages will be prepared in manuscript.

Hour, Date, Place	Summary of Events and Information	Remarks and references to Appendices
Oct. 16/15. MERICOURT.	Inspected 36 H. Bty. 104 Labour Bn. Report on letter to G.O.C.	
Oct. 17/15 "	Inspected 1st & 20th Bdes. Ammun. Col.	
Oct. 18/15 "	Office work.	
Oct. 19/15 "	Inspected 1/Welsh Regt. at M.V.S.	
Oct. 20/15 "	Inspected Div. Ammun. Col.	
Oct. 21/15. "	Inspected 2/Canadian G. Art. Held conference of all V.Os.	
Oct. 22/15 "	at M.V.S.	
Oct. 23/15 "	Inspected 1/Royal Scots.	
Oct. 24/15 "	Inspected 2/Canadian G. Art.	
Oct. 25/15 "	Officers chargers of Div. H.Qrs. left for new area. Rained all day	
Oct. 26/15 "	Proceeded to new area BOVELLES by car with A.D.M.S. Chargers arr. 2 p.m. Rained	
Oct 27/15 "	Inspected new site of M.V.S. Forge of 82nd Infantry Bde. Put Pte. ASHBY P.P.C.L.I. under arrest for ripping wall off repeated warnings. Sent report to his O.C. Rained all day	
Oct 28/15 "	Inspected A Bty & Ammun. Col. 1 & 9 Bde. Rained all day	
Oct 29/15.	Attended casting Board held by D.D.R. 3rd army.	

WAR DIARY
or
INTELLIGENCE SUMMARY.
(Erase heading not required.)

Army Form C. 2118.

Hour, Date, Place	Summary of Events and Information	Remarks and references to Appendices
Oct 30/15. BOVELLES.	Inspected 98 Bly. 82nd Field Amb.	
Oct 31/15. " "	Rained. Office work. Saw G.O.C.	

J.A. Roseley Major a.v.c.

121/7637

A.D.v.S. 27th Dn.

Nov. 1915

Vol VI

Army Form C. 2118.

WAR DIARY
or
INTELLIGENCE SUMMARY.
(Erase heading not required.)

Instructions regarding War Diaries and Intelligence Summaries are contained in F.S. Regs., Part II and the Staff Manual respectively. Title pages will be prepared in manuscript.

Hour, Date, Place	Summary of Events and Information	Remarks and references to Appendices
Nov. 1. 1915. BOVELLES.	Proceeded on leave.	
" 5 "	Returned from leave.	
" 6 "	Started mattening animals of the division prior to journey overseas.	
" 7 "	mattening	
" 8 & 9 "	mattening	
" 10 "	Completed the mattening	
" 11 "	Inspected M.V.S. of 131 Bty.	
" 12 "	Issued Circ. memo. No.10 attention directed to antivicious Horses on board ship & supply of medicines. Examining men for promotion to S.S.S. & Farr. Sgt.	
" 13 "	at M V.S.	
" 14 "	Issued Circ. memo. No 11 – re feeding prior to embarkation. Inspected A.T. Cable Coy. Inspected.	
" 15 "	Saw G.O.C. Signed.	
" 16 "	Inspected Hdqrs. Coy. Divisional Train.	
" 17 "	Inspected Div. Signal Coy. Office work.	
" 18 "	Held conference Officers A.V.C. Inspected 1st Bde R.F.A. Amm Col.	
" 19 "	Proceeded to railhead to inspect animals entrained by M.V.S.	

(73989) W4141—463. 400,000. 9/14. H.&J.Ltd. Forms/C. 2118/10.

WAR DIARY

or

~~INTELLIGENCE SUMMARY.~~

(Erase heading not required.)

Army Form C. 2118.

ADVS — 7 D

Hour, Date, Place	Summary of Events and Information	Remarks and references to Appendices
Nov. 20.1915. BOVELLES.	Inspected 51st Field Ambulance. 1/Royal Scots 17th Co. R.E.	
" 21 " "	Inspected Lieut. REID. A.V.C. evacuated sick.	
" 22 " "	Inspected 53rd Field Ambulance	
" 23 " "	at M.V.S.	
" 24 " "	Saw J.O.C. Office work. Lieut H. BIDLAKE. A.V.C joined advanced base to replace Lieut. REID. evacuated sick.	
" 25 " "	Lieut HUNTER proceeded to advanced base with Mobile Transport.	
" 26 " "	Capt. HALFHEAD went sick.	
" 27 " "	Inspected 96 Co. A.S.C.	
" 28 " "	Lieut. H.R. DAVIS. A.V.C. reported his arrival to replace Capt. Halfhead evacuated sick	
" 29 " "	Inspected 96 Coy. A.S.C.	
" 30 " "	at M.V.S. Saw D.O.C. office work.	

J. A. Nolan Major A.V.C.

Army Form C. 2118.

WAR DIARY
or
INTELLIGENCE SUMMARY.

(*Erase heading not required.*)

Instructions regarding War Diaries and Intelligence Summaries are contained in F.S. Regs., Part II. and the Staff Manual respectively. Title pages will be prepared in manuscript.

Hour, Date, Place	Summary of Events and Information	Remarks and references to Appendices

(73989) W4141—463. 400,000. 9/14. H.&J.Ltd. Forms/C. 2118/10.

Adv S 24 Dw
Dec
Vol VII

Army Form C. 2118.

WAR DIARY
or
INTELLIGENCE SUMMARY.
(Erase heading not required.)

Instructions regarding War Diaries and Intelligence Summaries are contained in F.S. Regs., Part II and the Staff Manual respectively. Title pages will be prepared in manuscript.

Hour, Date, Place			Summary of Events and Information	Remarks and references to Appendices
December 1.1915	BOVELLES		Mobile Vety. Section left for port of embarkation	
" 2	"	"	Inspecting survival Train.	
" 3	"	"	To Seux to inspect 2 horses left by 19th Bde R.F.A.	
" 4	"	"	Office work	
" 5	"	"	Inspected Surrey Yeomanry, 81st, 82nd & 3rd Field Ambulances.	
" 6	"	"	Collected horses from Seux.	
" 7	"	"	Left Bovelles	
" 8	"	"	In Train	
" 9	"	"	Arrived MARSEILLES.	
" 10	MARSEILLES	"	To Indian Vety. Hospital to arrange evacuation of sick.	
" 11	"	"	Rode round camp to note position of units	
" 12	"	"	Inspected 114 & 133 Batteries. Two cases of sarcoptic mange found in 133 Bty. Saw D.D.C. Arranged clipping & inspections	
" 13	"	"	Inspected 19th Bde R.F.A.	
" 14	"	"	Inspected 27th div. Signal Coy, 1st & 2nd Wessex R.E.	
" 15	"	"	Moved to BORELLY camp	
" 16	"	"	Inspected 81 & 82nd Infantry Brigade prior to embarkation at docks. Embarking.	

Army Form C. 2118.

WAR DIARY
or
INTELLIGENCE SUMMARY.
(Erase heading not required.)

Instructions regarding War Diaries and Intelligence Summaries are contained in F.S. Regs., Part II. and the Staff Manual respectively. Title pages will be prepared in manuscript.

Hour, Date, Place	Summary of Events and Information	Remarks and references to Appendices
Dec. 17th 1915 MARSEILLES	Capt ALLEN A.V.C. reported his arrival for duty in survision	
" 18 " "	Inspected 1st Bde R.F.A.	
" 19 " "	Inspecting site for new camps.	
" 20 " "	Inspected 133 Bty.	
" 21 " "	TO LA VALENTINE to inspect Infantry Transport.	
" 22 " "	At docks.	
" 23 " "	Inspected 114th Bty.	
" 24 " "	Office work.	
" 25 " "	Christmas Day.	
" 26 " "	Inspected R.E.	
" 27 " "	Inspected 133 Bty.	
" 28 " "	Inspected C. Bty & Ammn Col 129 Bde at Aubabin.	
" 29 " "	Lieut. H. BIRDRAKE A.V.C. left for England	
" 30 " "	Inspected M.M.P. div. H.Q. H.Q. R.E., & Signals &c	
" 31 " "	Arranging embarkation	

J.A. Moseley Major A.V.C.
A.D.V.S. 27 Div.

www.ingramcontent.com/pod-product-compliance
Lightning Source LLC
Chambersburg PA
CBHW082358170426
43191CB00048B/2065